Faith, Family, & Fun

Monthly Lessons to Color
and Connect with God's Love

Cathy D. Dudley

First Edition
ISBN: 978-0-578-48671-0
Library of Congress Control Number: 2019904453

Blessing2UPublishing
P.O. Box 854, Fincastle, VA 24090
Cover original artwork and lesson illustrations by Kyle Edgell
Printed in the United States of America
cathyddudley.com

This Book is Dedicated to Gary,
my wonderful husband,
who always has a spark of fun in his spirit.
I Love You, Honey!

A Big Thank You to Kyle Edgell,
my illustrator and art director,
who has captured so masterfully each expression
of our dear grandchildren
as they "star" in these stories.

From the Author

This delightful book was designed to help you and your family have a better connection with God—through faith in Jesus. Look inside. Flip through the pages. There's a lesson for every month of the year plus two holiday bonuses for Easter and Christmas. The unique lessons are ready to go with little or no preparation. And the charming caricature illustrations can be reproduced as coloring pages.

Each lesson begins with a real-life situation depicted in a black and white drawing. The brief story immediately captures children's attention as they too have moved to a new city, had a sleepover with cousins, or experienced the delight of a lost dog coming home. The lesson then takes a spiritual twist, becomes sprinkled with scripture and prayer, and concludes with some fun activities to support your family in growing in faith together.

Faith, Family, & Fun leads to special family memories. These memories are particularly meaningful because they're based on what really matters: the gospel. Your children will notice and soon be asking when you can have another family night. Now *this* is something to celebrate.

FUN FAMILY NIGHTS with a Focus on **Jesus!**

Love and Blessings,
Grammy Cathy

Another book by Cathy D. Dudley
TODDLER THEOLOGY - Childlike Faith for Everyone

CONTENTS

Lesson One 1
WHO'S WHO

Lesson Two 7
ALL POWERFUL

Lesson Three 13
A DECISION

Lesson Four 19
A WONDERFUL PROMISE

Lesson Five 25
A SPECIAL LAP

Lesson Six 31
A TICKET TO HEAVEN

Lesson Seven 37
WHAT REALLY MATTERS

Lesson Eight 43
BELIEVE IT ANYWAY

Lesson Nine 49
MAKING IT CLEAR

Lesson Ten 55
BEST FRIENDS

Lesson Eleven 61
ALWAYS THERE

Lesson Twelve 67
SOMEONE TO COUNT ON

Bonus Lesson for Easter 73
THE BEST SURPRISE EVER

Bonus Lesson for Christmas 79
HAPPY BIRTHDAY JESUS

WHO'S WHO

Last night I overheard Austin's Dad whispering to the man seated next to him. He was saying,"That's my son." I could hear the pride in his voice. Austin was receiving his baseball team's Good Sportsmanship Medal.

Can you think of a time when you heard one of your parents proudly pointing you out to a friend? Maybe it was at your dance recital or school's annual awards program. Did it make you feel happy inside knowing they were glad you belonged to them?

Well, guess who God's Son is? That's right — JESUS. Do you think God was proud of Jesus?

Listen to this story from the Bible:

> Jesus had grown up, and soon it would be time for Him to begin His ministry among the people. Jesus went to be baptized by John in the Jordan River. As soon as He came up out of the water, heaven was opened. Jesus saw the Spirit of God coming down like a dove and lighting on Him. Then a voice from heaven said, "This is my Son, whom I love; with Him I am well pleased."

God was claiming Jesus in front of everyone. Yes, God was proud of Him! I'm sure hearing His Father's voice made Jesus smile. He knew His Father would always be with Him. Jesus was now ready to start His three years of ministry, teaching and healing the people.

THE BIBLE TELLS ME SO

"As soon as Jesus was baptized, he went up out of the water. At that moment heaven was opened, and he saw the Spirit of God descending like a dove and lighting on him. And a voice from heaven said, 'This is my Son, whom I love; with him I am well pleased'" (Matthew 3:16-17, NIV).

PRAYER

Dear God, thank You for my family. I'm proud of each one. I pray You keep us in Your loving care now and always. Amen.

ACTIVITY

Look at your Family Tree, and trace how you're related to other members in your extended family. It's interesting to see how different generations connect with one another. Did you know your Daddy is your Grandpa's son? Now draw a BIG tree with lots of branches, and write family names on each limb.

EVERYDAY LIVING

Don't be shy to tell people who's who in your family. Be proud to introduce them to your friends. Have fun sharing stories about what you and your family do together. Family love is *very* special.

GOOD SPORTSMANSHIP
GATORS
G

ALL POWERFUL

Janey was jogging down the street when she heard someone yell, "Hi There, Sunshine!" She turned around and saw her best friend waving. Janey waved back flashing her sweet smile.

It's not unusual to give someone a name that describes their personality or character. Since Janey was always loving and kind, the name Sunshine fit her perfectly. Maybe you know a boy or girl whose nickname is Goofy because he or she likes to act silly.

Long ago, the Hebrews gave God many different names. They were trying to describe God's character. One name is Elohim which means Creator God. We read in Genesis 1:1, "In the beginning, God created the heavens and the earth."

My favorite Hebrew name for God is El Shaddai. It means the Almighty One who is all we need and has endless power to bless us. Listen to this miracle written in Exodus chapter 14. God parted the waters of the Red Sea. The Israelites could then escape the Egyptians by walking through the sea on dry land. Now that's powerful! Another time God blessed Abraham and his wife, Sarah, with a child. Sarah was 90 years old, and Abraham was 100. This miracle is recorded in the 21st chapter of Genesis.

These are just a few of the stories in the Bible telling about God's tremendous power. Yes, God has done countless great and wonderful things to help us throughout the ages. But remember God is still our El Shaddai today. For you see, absolutely *nothing* was—or is—impossible for God. God is indeed ALL powerful.

THE BIBLE TELLS ME SO

"I will proclaim your greatness, my God and King; I will thank you forever and ever. What you have done will be praised from one generation to the next; they will proclaim your mighty acts" (Psalm 145:1, 4, GNB).

PRAYER

Dear God, thank You for the miraculous and mighty ways You worked in the past. When I need help, remind me that ALL things are possible with You today too. I pray in the name of Jesus. Amen.

ACTIVITY

Sit down at a computer and Google the following phrase: meaning of the name ____________. Put your name in the blank. What does it say? Do you agree with the description? Does it sound like you? Now try this exercise with other family names.

EVERYDAY LIVING

Look around and count your blessings. Do you see any of God's miracles? Maybe it's a chirping bird, a snowflake, or a rainbow. And don't forget your sister, brother, or special playmate. What a great and powerful God we have! Let's give God all our thanks and praise.

A DECISION

When Cora Lou was in third grade, her family moved from Portland, Oregon, to Nashville, Tennessee. She had to be brave going to a new school, but every morning the same little girl smiled at her from across the classroom. After a week passed, she asked Cora Lou to sit with her at the lunch table. Soon they were chatting and laughing together like they'd known each other for years.

One day the little girl slipped Cora Lou a note at recess. It was folded in half twice. Cora Lou carefully opened the note and read, "Do you want to be my friend?" Below this sentence were two small boxes with the word *Yes* beside one and the word *No* beside the other. The instructions said to put a check in one of the squares, and then return the note. With a big smile, Cora Lou made a decision.

Jesus doesn't give us a note to check, but He does want to be our friend. How do we know this? In the Bible there's a scripture that talks about Jesus standing at the door and knocking. He wants you to open the door so He can come into your heart. I hope you decide YES!

THE BIBLE TELLS ME SO

"Behold, I stand at the door and knock; if anyone hears My voice and opens the door, I will come in to him, and will dine with him, and he with Me" (Revelation 3:20, NAS).

PRAYER

Dear Jesus, thank You for wanting to be my friend. Sometimes this is a bit puzzling since I can't see You. But it does make me smile. Help me to answer, "Yes", and show You that I'd like to be Your friend too. Amen.

ACTIVITY

Draw a BIG heart. The dictionary defines a friend as someone who likes you—who loves you—for who you are. Does this sound like Jesus? Write His name inside the heart. If you're still learning to spell, you can use connect-the-dot letters to print the word JESUS. Now write the names of other friends inside the heart. You can use a different color for each name. Cut out your heart, and tape it to the bathroom mirror. This picture will remind you that Jesus is your friend.

EVERYDAY LIVING

Show Jesus you want to be His friend. These are some ideas. Talk to Him in prayer. Praise Him with your singing. Be happy when it's Sunday, and you can go to church. Love Him by loving others. Serve Him by helping others.

Do you want to be my friend?
Yes
No
OR

A WONDERFUL PROMISE

What picture pops up in your mind when you tell someone you're going home? Do you live in a neighborhood with paved sidewalks and houses with neat yards? Do you live down a dirt road crowded with metal shacks? Do you live on a farm where the nearest house is half a mile away? Do you live in a big city with lots of apartments and row houses?

You might really like the place where you live, or maybe you wish you could move. Either way is OK because your today home is just temporary. That means it's just for now.

Listen to this story from the book of John:

> Jesus' disciples knew He was leaving soon. Jesus didn't want them to be sad. So He told them He would prepare a place for them where He was going. Jesus said it would be in His Father's house.

This wonderful promise is for us today too. We each have a forever home waiting for us in heaven. What a special gift! We can only dream what it'll be like, but I'm thinking it will be everything you're hoping for and *more*. Remember—Jesus ALWAYS keeps His promises.

THE BIBLE TELLS ME SO

"In my Father's house are many mansions; if it were not so, I would have told you. I go to prepare a place for you" (John 14:2, KJV).

PRAYER

Dear Jesus, I can't wait to see the home You've made for me in heaven. Thank You for this wonderful promise. I love You! Amen.

ACTIVITY

Get a realtor magazine that has descriptions of homes for sale in your area. There are usually photographs of the houses too. Cut out your favorite, and glue it in the middle of a sheet of paper. Pretend this is your home in heaven. Use your imagination, and finish the picture any way you want.

EVERYDAY LIVING

When you tell someone you're going to do something, be sure to do it! Even if you don't use the word promise, you want everybody to know they can count on you. This is an important part of who we should be as God's children.

A SPECIAL LAP

Naomi paused to rub her sleepy eyes. She was playing on the floor with her little ponies. Watching from her rocking chair, Grammy crocheted nearby. Naomi tenderly put the last baby pony to bed and slowly climbed into Grammy's lap. They rocked together silently until Naomi fell asleep.

Sitting in the driveway, Dad was sanding a bookcase when he saw the accident. Super Sawyer was going too fast on his skateboard. When he hit a bump in the sidewalk, there was a big crash, and his board went lying through the air! Sobbing, Sawyer ran over and plopped into Dad's lap. He pulled up his pants to show two bloody knees. Dad's comforting words and a few band-aids soon made everything alright again.

Have you noticed when someone wants to sit on another's lap, there's a special connection between them? Well, when Jesus walked on earth years ago, that's exactly the way it was between Him and the children. Jesus *knew* each child was special, and the children felt the same way about Him.

In the book of Matthew, the Bible tells us about a day when Jesus was ministering to a large crowd. He was teaching and healing the sick. There were so many people that His disciples tried to stop the children from coming to Him. When Jesus saw what was happening, He said, "Let the children come to me." No matter how busy Jesus was, He always made time for children. They would laugh together as He took them in His arms.

Jesus thinks YOU are special too! Can you imagine sitting on Jesus' lap and hearing His stories?

THE BIBLE TELLS ME SO

"Jesus said, 'Let the children come to me and do not stop them, because the kingdom of heaven belongs to such as these'" (Matthew 19:14, GNB).

PRAYER

Dear Jesus, I love this story in the Bible about You and the children. It tells me I'm important and special to You. Thank You. Amen.

ACTIVITY

Draw a stick figure of yourself. Use a circle for your head. Attach short lines for your neck and two arms, and connect longer lines for your body and two legs. Put two dots for your eyes and a curved line for your smiling mouth. Now add as much detail as you'd like. Write your name under the picture, and print this sentence: Jesus thinks I'm special!

EVERYDAY LIVING

When you're sitting on a favorite lap at bedtime, ask that person to tell you which Jesus story he or she likes best. You'll be surprised at all the different ones. Then decide which story *you* like best.

A TICKET TO HEAVEN

Have you ever lied and told your Mother you didn't eat the missing cookie? Have you ever hit your brother or sister because he or she wouldn't stop splashing you in the pool? Or maybe you said something mean to one of your friends. These are all examples of ways we sin.

A sin is something wrong you do, say, or sometimes just think. It's not that you plan to behave badly. It just happens. You see, we're all born with a sinful nature. That means we have a built-in urge to think of ourselves first.

This sinning causes serious problems. It breaks our good connection with God because God wants us to love one another. And yes, sin keeps us out of heaven where no bad thing is allowed. All this makes us sad. Yet we keep sinning—slipping up and doing things we shouldn't. We can't help it.

No one can be good all the time.

But there's Good News! God has given us a Savior. His name is JESUS. And Jesus loves us so much that He went along with His Father God's plan to save us from our sins. That's right. Jesus died on the cross for the forgiveness of our sins: yesterday's, today's, and tomorrow's too.

The word forgive means to forget and remember no more. So it's like the blood of Jesus erases our sins and buys us all tickets to heaven. Now *this* is something to celebrate!

THE BIBLE TELLS ME SO

"For God so loved the world that he gave his one and only Son, that whoever believes in him shall not perish but have eternal life" (John 3:16, NIV).

PRAYER

Dear Jesus, my Savior, thank You for dying on the cross for me. Because of You my sins are forgiven, and I can have my very own ticket to heaven. I love You! Amen.

ACTIVITY

Find a blackboard. Draw a picture of a dark cloud, or write the word SIN. Now erase your work. This is what forgiveness of your sins looks like. They are gone! It's like they never happened. You can do this activity over and over and over again to help you remember that God will always forgive your sins: yesterday's, today's, and tomorrow's too.

EVERYDAY LIVING

When you pray, you can ask God to forgive your sins and know for sure they're erased. They're forgotten. What a wonderful feeling! Some people even pray, "For Jesus' sake, forgive my sins." They are remembering what Jesus did on the cross and reminding themselves that Jesus is the Savior of the world.

WHAT REALLY MATTERS

Thanksgiving Day in our city means it's time for the Drumstick Dash. This is an annual downtown event to raise money for our homeless neighbors. Austin and Janey had jogged around the last corner and finished the race in record time. Naomi and Cora Lou had walked, skipped, cartwheeled, and danced along the course. With their dogs on leashes, Leo and Sawyer had stopped every block or two to check out the trees.

How it happens doesn't matter. What really matters is crossing the finish line. Christians often talk about God's gift of salvation. Salvation means we have a forever home in heaven because Jesus died on the cross for our sins. Well, guess what? God planned it all. That's right. And God freely gives us this salvation. There's nothing we can do to earn or deserve it. That's how much God loves us! Grace is the word that's used to describe God's amazing love.

Now a gift isn't really yours until you take hold of it. So faith is when *you* accept God's wonderful gift of salvation and believe in Jesus and His story. How awesome to know you have a ticket to heaven! Yes, this faith thing is very, very important.

The Bible tells us God's Holy Spirit is always at work when faith is growing. But it's also very personal and doesn't happen in exactly the same way for any two people. Sometimes a faith journey starts when a baby is baptized. Sometimes it begins as a tiny seed when a child is brought to church. And sometimes faith is like a light bulb that suddenly turns on when someone first understands how much God loves them. These are only three of the many ways a person might come to believe.

How it happens doesn't matter. What really matters is YOU BELIEVING in Jesus and His story.

FOR THE BIBLE TELLS ME SO

"For it is by God's grace that you have been saved by faith. It is not the results of your own efforts, but God's gift, so that no one can boast about it" (Ephesians 2:8-9, GNB).

PRAYER

Dear God, I love You. Thank You for Your Holy Spirit in my life to draw me ever closer to Jesus and stay focused on what really matters. Amen.

ACTIVITY

Go on a hike, or just walk around your house. Look through a pair of binoculars at an object far away. At first the object appears blurry. Keep looking as you turn the focusing ring. The edges of the object will become sharp. This is the way the Holy Spirit helps us believe and clearly see the love of God.

EVERYDAY LIVING

Having a friend over to spend the night is a fun adventure. But sometimes after playing hard and eating snacks, even the best of friends disagree at bedtime. What if you like to sleep in a dark room and your friend needs a night light? Would you insist on having your own way? What would Jesus do? This is the perfect time to ask yourself, "What really matters?"

DRUMSTICK
move your feet so others can eat
DASH
DRUMSTICK
DASH
DRUMSTICK
DASH
DRUMSTICK
DASH
DRUMSTICK
DASH

BELIEVE IT ANYWAY

Life is full of mysteries. Mysteries are things we can't fully explain or understand. Mixing red and blue paint together makes a lovely purple color. To me, this is a mystery. I can't explain all the details, but I believe it anyway. Instantly receiving a picture or text message from hundreds of miles away is another mystery to me. How can this be? I can't explain all the details, but I believe it anyway.

In the Bible, the Jesus story is called the Good News of the gospel. It's also sometimes referred to as God's mystery. I guess it is pretty unbelievable that the Son of God could be born of a woman. And what about the part where Jesus died on the cross? His blood erases all our sins and buys us tickets to heaven. How can this be? Then there's the resurrection miracle when Jesus didn't stay dead. On the first Easter long ago, our Savior rose from the grave! Before He ascended back into heaven, Jesus was actually seen walking and talking again with His disciples.

Wow, no one can explain all the details of how these things happened. Only God can do that. Believe it anyway. That's called having faith. The dictionary defines faith as believing in someone or something with complete confidence when there's often little or no proof. This can be hard. But when we're talking about faith in Jesus, God promises to give us the Holy Spirit to help us believe.

Here's the bottom line. I'm thinking Jesus may just be the most amazing mystery ever! We can't fully explain or understand all the Bible tells us about Him, but I'm believing it anyway. How about you?

FOR THE BIBLE TELLS ME SO

"What we see now is like a dim image in a mirror; then we shall see face-to-face. What I know now is only partial; then it will be complete, as complete as God's knowledge of me" (1 Corinthians 13:12, GNB).

PRAYER

Heavenly Father, thank You for giving the world Jesus. He's Your Son and our Savior. The Bible also says He's Your mystery. Please help me be content with some unanswered questions until I meet You face-to-face. And for now, increase Your Holy Spirit within me so that I can say with confidence, "I believe!" In Jesus' name I pray. Amen.

ACTIVITY

Mix red and blue paint together. Were you surprised to see purple? I can't explain how this new color appeared. To me, it's a beautiful mystery. Draw a cross and paint it with your new color.

EVERYDAY LIVING

Visit a Ripley's Believe It or Not Museum (or Google it). This is a place that presents strange exhibits and tells such unusual stories that people have trouble believing them. I guess you could say it's a museum of mysteries. Everyone must decide for themselves whether to believe it anyway.

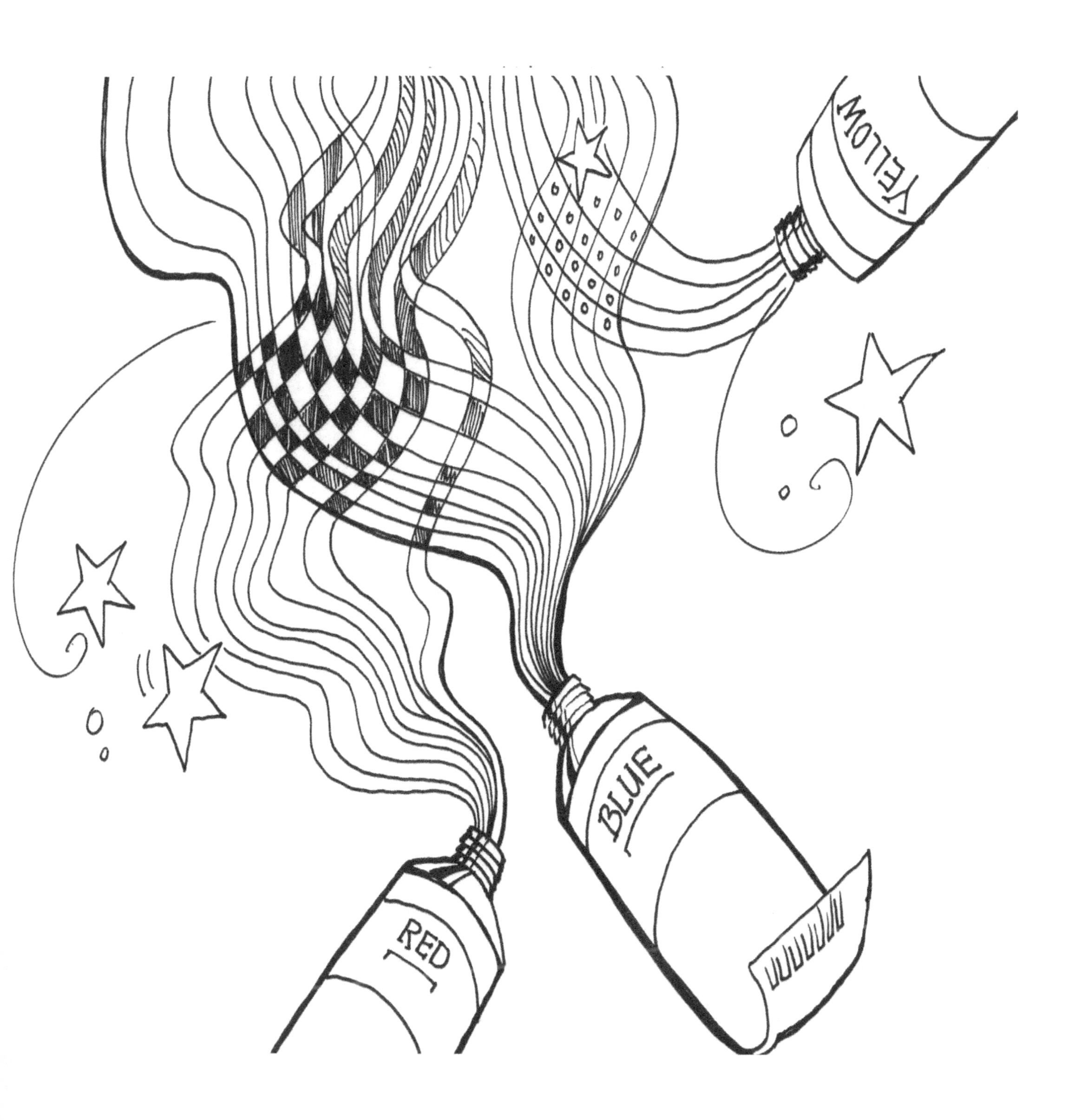
YELLOW
BLUE
RED

MAKING IT CLEAR

Grandpa was frowning as he read the instruction manual for the third time. He had purchased an answering machine for his phone and was having trouble understanding the technical language. The words seemed like nonsense, and he was getting more and more frustrated.

At last he decided to call the helpline. Within minutes the IT specialist made all the directions clear, and Grandpa had the new system working perfectly.

God gave us Jesus. There are many stories in the Bible describing the things Jesus did and explaining why God sent Him to earth. Sometimes even Bible scholars don't comprehend everything or agree on what all the words mean.

But God also sent us the Holy Spirit. The Holy Spirit is ten times better than any IT specialist in the world! He helps you understand the Jesus story and His gift of salvation. With the Holy Spirit, God's message of love becomes clear.

THE BIBLE TELLS ME SO

"We have not received the spirit of the world but the Spirit who is from God, that we may understand what God has freely given us" (1 Corinthians 2:12, NIV).

PRAYER

Dear God, thank You for sending me the Holy Spirit, my helper in understanding just how much You and Jesus love me. Amen.

ACTIVITY

Make a pencil rubbing picture. Choose a flat but slightly raised object. This is the image you will transfer onto your paper. Good examples are a coin, a key, or a guitar pick. Don't show what it is. Now place a blank, white piece of paper over your object. Holding your pencil at an angle, rub the side of the pencil lead back and forth over the surface of the object until the picture begins to appear. Try not to let the paper slip. Is your picture becoming clear? Can anyone guess what it is?

EVERYDAY LIVING

The drive home from church is a great time to talk about the Sunday sermon. Never be embarrassed to ask what the words mean. The more you understand about the Jesus story, the closer you'll feel to Him.

OPERATING
INSTRUCTIONS

BEST FRIENDS

Leo and Sawyer are cousins, and their friendship is very special. They like to tell people they're best friends. When their families visit one another, the strong love they share is undeniable. They build with Legos, dress up for amazing battles with their pretend swords, and do lots of fun things together. But Leo and Sawyer live in different states—so many miles apart that they only see each other twice a year. As you can imagine, when it's time to head home, the boys hug one another tightly and yell, "NO, don't go!"

Jesus loves all the children in the world and is their friend. That means He's *your* friend too. Just like Leo and Sawyer, it's exciting to think of you and Jesus doing all sorts of fun things together.

Well, guess what? Jesus never has to go home. That's right. Jesus is always with you! And I bet the joy He brings will make whatever you're doing even better.

I know you can't see Jesus, but the Bible tells us He's walking by our side. Jesus IS real. He's as real as the invisible wind that lifts your kite into the sky. And He loves being with you, doing whatever you're doing. Jesus smiles when you laugh, sends help when you cry, and protects you when you're afraid. Doesn't that sound like a best friend?

THE BIBLE TELLS ME SO

"...And I will be with you always, to the end of the age" (Matthew 28:20, GNB).

PRAYER

Dear Jesus, thank You for being my forever friend. I know You're real, and I can't wait to do things together! Amen.

ACTIVITY

Fly a kite to remind you that the wind is there even though you can't see it. And even though you can't see Jesus, He's right there too, sharing in your fun.

EVERYDAY LIVING

There are many hymns and poems that talk about Jesus walking with us through life. Two of my favorites are "In the Garden" and "Footprints." Find the words, and sing or read them aloud. They paint a beautiful picture of you and Jesus.

ALWAYS THERE

Cora Lou loves it when her two cousins, Janey and Naomi, spend the night. After dinner, they have a silly dance party. Then they look for shooting stars from the back porch. What fun!

When it's bedtime, they spread out their sleeping bags in Cora Lou's room and whisper back and forth. Cora Lou likes it best when it's her turn to sleep in the middle. This is such a cozy spot; it's perfect for hearing every word of their shared secrets. And if she wakes up in the night, she isn't afraid.

Waking up in a dark room is scary for a lot of children. They think they're all alone. But remember—Jesus made a promise to His disciples to be with them ALWAYS.

Jesus' promise is true for us today too. That means every hour of the day or darkest night, He's right there beside you. Even though you can't see your stuffed animal lovie, you know it's laying by your side, right? Well, Jesus is there too!

Just whisper the name *Jesus*. He hears, and you'll feel better quicker than you can reach out and hug your favorite lovie.

THE BIBLE TELLS ME SO

"Even when I walk through the darkest valley, I will not be afraid, for you are close beside me" (Psalm 23:4, NLT).

PRAYER

Dear Jesus, Thank You for always being by my side. I love You! Amen.

ACTIVITY

Play a Guessing Game. Line up a row of 5 small items on the table. You can use things like a matchbox car, a marble, a penny, a hair clip, and a life saver. Now take turns covering one item with a cup while the other person isn't looking. He or she has to guess what's hidden. Remove the cup to prove it's still there even though you couldn't see it.

EVERYDAY LIVING

Ask people to tell you one thing they know is there even though it's invisible. How about the warmth of the sun? Others might say music, the wind, love, or the taste of something sweet.

SOMEONE TO COUNT ON

When Austin was a little boy, things didn't always go his way. Maybe he didn't eat enough dinner to get dessert. Maybe he drew that awful Chutes and Ladders card that sent his game piece sliding back down to a square on the first row. Or maybe he was too young to ride bikes with the neighborhood gang.

These were times Austin felt sorry for himself. He thought no one cared. He would go upstairs to his bedroom and complain to his dog, Gus, "Nobody loves me—Everybody hates me—Guess I'll go eat worms." These are silly words from a childhood song, but they fit his mood perfectly. Have you heard it?

Well, today Austin is eleven years old. Things still don't always go his way. But now Austin knows something wonderful that helps him. Listen to this. There's someone you can count on to love you, even if it seems like not one person in the whole world cares. That someone is JESUS.

I bet you know the beloved song,"Jesus Loves Me." It was written for *all* God's children, no matter how old you are, and reminds us that His love for us is eternal. That means it's always, always there and never ends.

So the next time you're feeling down and think no one cares, try humming this chorus, "Yes, Jesus loves me—Yes, Jesus loves me—Yes, Jesus loves me—The Bible tells me so." I know the corners of your mouth will soon be smiling again.

THE BIBLE TELLS ME SO

"Neither the world above nor the world below—there is nothing in all creation that will ever be able to separate us from the love of God which is ours through Christ Jesus our Lord" (Romans 8:39, GNB).

PRAYER

Dear Jesus, thank You for loving me at all times. Help me remember this if I ever think no one in the whole world cares. I know You're there to listen to my problems and lift my spirits. What a wonderful feeling! Amen.

ACTIVITY

Make a pile of worms from playdough. Use them to spell out the name JESUS. Then sing the song, "Jesus Loves Me."

EVERYDAY LIVING

There are many greeting cards in stores. Hallmark is a well known brand. Guideposts also has a line of cards: Someone Cares. They're suggesting that sending cards lets people know you truly care about them. I agree. The two words, SOMEONE CARES, are even printed on the back of their greeting cards. What a great motto! So when you know a friend could use a little pick me up, why not make a special card for him or her? You can create your own message or simply write *someone cares.*

THE BEST SURPRISE EVER

Has anything so wonderful ever happened to you that it was hard to believe? Maybe your parents told you the family was going to Disney World for your summer vacation, and that's exactly where you went in June. Or maybe your dog was lost for a whole week, and then he suddenly came home.

Well, on the very first Easter long ago, some women went to Jesus' tomb on Sunday morning. It was three days after Jesus had been crucified. They saw the big stone at the entrance had been rolled away. When they looked inside, only His linen grave clothes were laying there. Wow, they couldn't believe their eyes. Jesus' body was gone! Instead an angel was standing there, reminding them that Jesus had said He would be raised back to life in three days.

Now they knew it was true. Jesus was *alive* again. His friends were a little afraid but mostly just very, very happy. They ran to tell His disciples that He is risen!

Years later, Christians all over the world still greet one another on Easter Sunday with these same three words: HE IS RISEN.

THE BIBLE TELLS ME SO

"The angel spoke to the women. 'You must not be afraid, he said. I know you are looking for Jesus, who was crucified. He is not here; He has been raised, just as he said. Come here and see the place where He was lying'" (Matthew 28:5-6, GNB).

PRAYER

Dear Jesus, I love hearing the Easter story over and over again. I'm glad You didn't stay dead. Some people think it's too amazing to be true, but I know You're alive. ALLELUIA and Amen.

ACTIVITY

An egg is a symbol of new life. So at Easter time—or anytime—you can celebrate that Jesus was raised from the dead by coloring a hard boiled egg. Use *lots* of bright colors to remind you how happy Jesus' friends were long ago. And we're happy today too. Jesus is alive!

EVERYDAY LIVING

Here's a challenge. When you read a book, decide if it's a made up story like a fairy tale. Or is it a true story like the Easter one in the Bible?

LOST
DOG

HAPPY BIRTHDAY JESUS

Leo joined the other boys and girls sitting in a circle on the floor. Mrs. Stanley, their teacher, had her pen and paper. She was writing down beside each name their answer to this question, "What date were you born?"

When everyone had taken a turn, Mrs. Stanley smiled and announced they were now ready to make a class Birthday Calendar. There was lots of excitement as balloon stickers were added. Leo's favorite part was sprinkling sparkle glitter over the whole poster *and* himself. Then the calendar was hung with care beside the blackboard so all the children could see what special days they'd be celebrating.

There's a lot of excitement at Christmastime too. Christmas is one of the most special of all birthdays. Do you know who was born on this day? That's right—JESUS. Although the Bible doesn't tell us the exact month and day of Jesus' birthday, many years ago some church officials decided to celebrate it on December 25th. And now it's become the most wonderful time of the year!

The beautiful story of Jesus' nativity is written in the Bible. Nativity is a fancy word that means birth. In Luke chapter 2, we read about singing angels appearing to shepherds who were keeping watch over their flock by night. The angels were praising God and proclaiming the birth of a Savior, Christ the Lord, in Bethlehem. When the angels went back up into heaven, the shepherds hurried off and found their way to Mary, Joseph, and the newborn baby lying in a manger. What an awesome night that was! It reminds me of one of my favorite Christmas carols, "Joy to the World, the Lord is Come."

We learn a little more about the Jesus story in Matthew chapter 2. It tells of visitors from the East who saw Jesus' star and followed it. These men are sometimes called the three kings or the three wise men. They traveled miles and miles, riding on camels, each bringing a gift to Jesus.

And this is how the birth of Jesus Christ took place on the very first Christmas long ago. Happy Birthday, Jesus!

THE BIBLE TELLS ME SO

"for today in the city of David there has been born for you a Savior, who is Christ the Lord. This will be a sign for you: you will find a baby wrapped in cloths and lying in a manger" (Luke 2:11-12, NAS).

PRAYER

Dear God, when Christmastime comes, I'm so excited about Santa, our Christmas tree, and presents to open. Help me pause and remember that You gave us the BEST gift of all. You sent us Jesus on the very first Christmas. Thank You! Amen.

ACTIVITY

Many Christmas decorations remind us of things that happened on that holy night when Jesus was born. So how about making some ornaments for your tree? If it's not Christmas now, you can pack them away until the time is right.

Here's the RECIPE for Baking Soda White Clay Christmas Ornaments.

Ingredients:

1¼ cups baking soda, ¾ cup cornstarch, and ¾ cup cold water.

Mix together the baking soda and cornstarch in a saucepan. Add the water, and cook over medium heat about 10 minutes stirring constantly. When the clay thickens and is the consistency of mashed potatoes, turn it out onto a plate to cool for 15 minutes. Now pat the clay gently, and roll it out on wax paper to approximately ¼ inch thick. Make shapes with cookie cutters. Near the top of each shape, use a straw to poke a hole. These decorations must dry at least 24 hours. Turn them over occasionally. When both sides are completely dry, you're ready to paint the ornaments or add glitter over a thin layer of glue. For hanging, thread strings through the holes.

EVERYDAY LIVING

Find a cozy place in your home to display the manger scene all year long. If your friends ask you about it, you can tell them the Christmas story. You can also teach them one of your favorite Christmas carols.

Birthdays!
JAN
FEB
MARCH
APRIL
MAY
JUNE
JULY
AUGUST
SEPT
OCT
NOV
DEC

GOD BLESS YOU!

Cathy D. Dudley

lives in the Blue Ridge Mountains of Virginia with her husband, Gary. She thanks God for giving her the words to write and invites you to visit cathyddudley.com.

People are Saying

"This is the perfect book for sharing God's love with a child. It's uplifting and encouraging with wonderful stories, prayers, and activities."
Lisa L. Bennett, President / Founder VictoryNOW Films and TV, Executive Producer Grace Film Project

"Incredibly Unique! This creative book presents the gospel in such down-to-earth ways that children will be drawn closer to Jesus and His love for them."
Sam Sorbo, American actress, talk radio host, and co-author with husband Kevin of *Share the Light*

"Having taught children for thirty-five years, I personally welcome this fresh offering. Each chapter connects the reader to a concept that will enhance their belief system."
Pastor David Cox, President Virginia Weekday Religious Education Assoc., Inc.

"An easily relatable book, recommended for the kitchen table and anywhere families gather, share, and learn … engaging the young and the young at heart along their faith journey!"
Rev. Keith A. Olivier, Chaplain, Virginia Lutheran Homes, Inc.

"This excellent resource will unite families with each other and to Jesus in a meaningful way."
Barbara Baranowski, Director of Roanoke Valley Christian Writers

"In this book's charm and liveliness, it is a wonderful foundation for Christian story-telling encouraging the development of the love of Jesus Christ."
Dikkon Eberhart, author of the popular Christian memoir, *The Time Mom Met Hitler, Frost Came to Dinner, and I Heard the Greatest Story Ever Told*

"This book brings together all the elements of Jesus' words … 'let the children come unto me.' Through engaging stories and artwork, children and adults alike are invited into life-changing conversation."
Lee Clark, CEO Rescue Mission of Roanoke, Inc.

"Thank you, Cathy, for helping families develop a culture of discipleship in their homes and for leaving a spiritual inheritance to us all through this new work!"
Eric Gutierrez, Licensed Minister, Licensed Professional Counselor, Christian School Administrator

Made in the USA
Las Vegas, NV
03 November 2021